AN IMAGINATION LIBRARY SERIES

Colors of the Sea
CORAL REEF FEEDERS

Eric Ethan and Marie Bearanger

Gareth Stevens Publishing
MILWAUKEE

For a free color catalog describing Gareth Stevens Publishing's list of high-quality books and multimedia programs, call 1-800-542-2595 (USA) or 1-800-461-9120 (Canada). Gareth Stevens Publishing's Fax: (414) 225-0377.
See our catalog, too, on the World Wide Web: http://gsinc.com

Library of Congress Cataloging-in-Publication Data

Ethan, Eric.
    Coral reef feeders / Eric Ethan and Marie Bearanger.
      p. cm. — (Colors of the sea)
    Includes index.
    Summary: Presents information about the various sea creatures that feed on coral polyps and algae of the coral reef, including fish, snails, slugs, and starfish.
    ISBN 0-8368-1738-9 (lib. bdg.)
     1. Coral reef animals—Food—Juvenile literature. 2. Coral reef ecology—Juvenile literature. [1. Coral reef animals. 2. Coral reefs and islands. 3. Coral reef ecology. 4. Ecology.] I. Bearanger, Marie. II. Title. III. Series: Ethan, Eric. Colors of the sea.
QL125.E83   1997
577.7'89—dc21   96-37056

First published in North America in 1997 by
Gareth Stevens Publishing
1555 North RiverCenter Drive, Suite 201
Milwaukee, WI 53212 USA

This edition © 1997 by Gareth Stevens, Inc. Adapted from *Colors of the Sea* © 1992 by Elliott & Clark Publishing, Inc., Washington, D.C. Text by Owen Andrews. Photographs © 1992 by W. Gregory Brown. Additional end matter © 1997 by Gareth Stevens, Inc.

Text: Eric Ethan, Marie Bearanger
Page layout: Eric Ethan, Helene Feider
Cover design: Helene Feider
Series design: Shari Tikus

The publisher wishes to acknowledge the encouragement and support of Glen Fitzgerald.

Printed in the United States of America

1 2 3 4 5 6 7 8 9 01 00 99 98 97

TABLE OF CONTENTS

STURDY, STONE HOMES

Coral is made of a hard substance called **limestone**. Tiny animals known as coral **polyps** make the limestone shells or skeletons for use as their homes.

But coral polyps are not safe from **predators** in their sturdy, stone homes. They are eaten by various sea creatures, including fish, sea snails, starfish, and sponges. The polyps are a good source of **protein** for these creatures.

The queen angelfish, *Holocanthus ciliarus*, is common around coral reefs. It feeds on the sea creatures living there.

HOW DO FISH EAT CORAL?

Fish that prey on coral polyps are divided into two basic groups — polyp-nippers and **algae**-scrapers. These fish have special mouths that allow them to reach the polyps.

Butterflyfish are polyp-nippers that swim through the nooks and crannies of coral reefs. They have special pointed mouths that allow them to poke into the coral and pull out the polyps. Stinging cells on the **tentacles** of the coral polyps do not harm butterflyfish.

The masked butterflyfish, *Chaetodon semilarvatus*, has a pointed triangle-shaped mouth for feeding on coral polyps.

The longnose filefish is another type of coral polyp-nipper. The filefish's mouth is at the end of a long nose. The mouth and nose are perfectly shaped for pulling coral polyps and other small creatures from their hiding places.

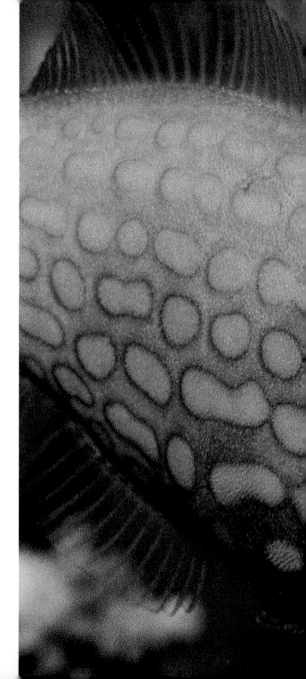

The longnose filefish, *Oxymonocanthus longirostris*, feeds on the polyps of a type of coral called staghorn coral.

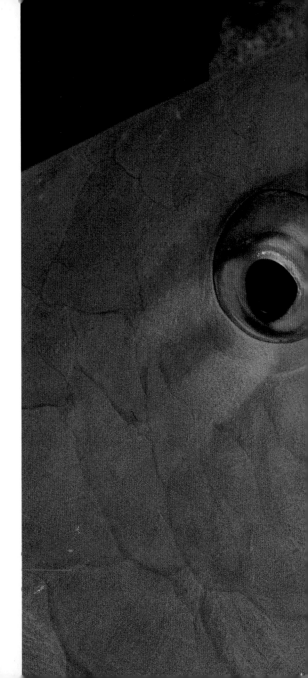

Algae-scrapers feed on the algae that covers parts of coral. One type of algae-scraper is the parrotfish. With its strong jaws and two sets of teeth, it bites off chunks of coral and grinds the chunks into sand. Then it sucks out the **nutrients** from the algae and passes the sand through its body. A parrotfish can make up to 5 pounds (2.3 kilograms) of sand a day.

The jaws and teeth of the ember parrotfish, *Scarus rubroviolaceus*, are very strong for biting off chunks of coral.

CORAL REEF HOMES

Fish that feed on coral never go far from their food supply. Butterflyfish often pair off and settle in one part of a reef. They patrol their chosen area, looking for food. Their bright colors warn other fish that the area is taken.

The coral reef also provides angelfish and parrot-fish with shelter. Coral has many hiding places. When predators come looking for them, these fish quickly hide in the coral.

The French angelfish, *Pomocanthus paru*, feeds on soft coral and hides from predators in the reef.

Instead of simply hiding in the coral reef, many sea creatures dig into the coral. Small sponges called cliona use chemicals found in their bodies to dig into living and dead coral. Certain sea creatures, such as date mussels and snails, create homes for themselves by boring holes in the coral.

Sometimes areas of a coral reef have so many holes bored into it by sea creatures that the reef falls apart. Scientists believe these creatures are responsible for half of all reef **erosion**.

These are the eyes of a spider conch, *Lambis crocata*. It hides below the reef, feeding on algae.

WHAT ARE NUDIBRANCHS?

Nudibranchs are sea creatures that are also known as slugs or sea snails. They do not have shells, and their soft bodies come in many forms. Most are between 1/2 inch (1 centimeter) and 3 inches (7.5 cm) long.

In the Greek language, the name *nudibranch* means "naked gills." A nudibranch does not have a stomach. Instead, it has a **radula**, which is a kind of ribbon of teeth. When a nudibranch crawls across coral, its radula scrapes off small chunks of the polyps and algae it touches.

Top: The ocellated nudibranch, *Phyllidia ocellata,* feeds on sponges.

Bottom: The chromodorid nudibranch, *Chromodoris,* is found at depths of 30-90 feet (9-27 meters).

Even though nudibranchs have soft bodies and move slowly, they are not eaten by other animals. This is because they taste unpleasant to the animals.

Nudibranchs eat coral polyps even though the polyps' tentacles contain stinging **cells**. Nudibranchs not only eat these cells, but they **recycle** them into stinging cells on their own backs. This is another way in which nudibranchs are protected from predators.

Top: The ruffle-backed slug, *Triadachia crispata*, is a nudibranch found in shallow waters.

Bottom: The flamingo tongue nudibranch, *Cyphoma gibbosum*, is a slug that leaves a dark trail behind where its radula has scraped polyps off sea fan coral.

WHAT ARE STARFISH?

There are over 1,500 kinds of starfish. They feed on coral polyps. All starfish have at least five arms, and a few types have more. Starfish move by pulling themselves along the surface of the coral with their arms. They accomplish this with the use of small **suction** cups that cover the underside of their arms. Their mouths are located at the very center of the underside of their bodies.

Most starfish reach 4-12 inches (10-30 cm) across. One rare species, *Medgardia xandaros*, grows to over 3 feet (90 cm) across.

Sea star, *Fromia monilis*, is a type of starfish found near coral reefs.

Starfish have very few predators. This is because their top side is covered in tough, armored skin. In addition, starfish do not taste very good to other animals. Because starfish have few enemies, they can **overpopulate** coral reefs. When this happens, damage is done to the reefs by the starfish because of overfeeding.

Starfish have the unusual ability to regrow an arm if one is lost. In fact, they can regrow an entire body from one arm and a small part of their central disk. Starfish have one other unusual feature. At the end of each arm is a spot similar to an eye. But starfish move mainly by touch, not sight.

GLOSSARY

algae (AL-jee) — Living water plants that are food for many sea creatures.

cell (SELL) — The smallest and most basic part of all living beings.

erosion (e-RO-zshun) — The process of being worn away, especially by wind or water.

limestone (LIME-stone) — A calcium carbonate crystalline shell or skeleton secreted by coral polyps. The substance is hard and stony and protects the polyp.

nudibranch (NU-dah-brank) — A sea animal (also called a mollusk) that does not have a shell, gills, or a stomach.

nutrient (NU-tree-ent) — The part of food needed by living beings to survive.

overpopulate (oh-ver-POP-yu-late) — To become crowded with too many beings.

polyp (PAH-lip) — A small animal that lives in the water; it has a tube-shaped body, a mouth surrounded by tentacles, and a limestone shell or skeleton.

predator (PRED-a-ter) — An animal that lives by eating other animals.

protein (PRO-teen) — A substance found in all living beings that is necessary to life.

radula (RAD-yu-lah) — The ribbon of tiny teeth of certain mollusks.

recycle (ree-SY-cuhl) — To change the makeup of an item and use it again.

suction (SUK-shun) — A force created by removing part of the air that is present. Sea creatures use suction to attach themselves to a surface.

tentacle (TENT-ah-cuhl) — A flexible, tubelike arm of a sea creature that is used for collecting food, holding, moving, or stinging.

WEB SITES

http://www.blacktop.com/coralforest/

http://planet-hawaii.com/sos/coralreef.html

PLACES TO WRITE

The Cousteau Society, Inc.
870 Greenbrier Circle, Suite 402
Chesapeake, VA 23320

Environmental Protection Agency
Oceans and Coastal Protection Division
401 M Street SW
Washington, D.C. 20460

Greenpeace (USA)
1436 U Street NW
Washington, D.C. 20009

Greenpeace (Canada)
2623 West Fourth Avenue
Vancouver, British Columbia V6K 1P8

Greenpeace Foundation
185 Spadina Avenue, Sixth Floor
Toronto, Ontario M5T 2C6

Center for Marine Conservation
1725 DeSales Street, Suite 500
Washington, D.C. 20036

National Geographic Society
17th and M Streets NW
Washington, D.C. 20036

INDEX